spells to

spells to change your life

Little Books by Big Names™

First published in the United Kingdom in 2003 by Little Books Ltd,
48 Catherine Place, London SW1E 6HL

10 9 8 7 6 5 4 3 2

Text copyright © 2003 by Lois Bourne
Design and layout copyright © 2003 by Little Books Ltd
Illustrations © by Steve Crisp

A CIP catalogue record for this book is available from the British Library.

ISBN: 1 904435 10 6

The author and publisher will be grateful for any information that will
assist them in keeping future editions up-to-date. Although all reasonable care
has been taken in the preparation of this book, neither the publisher, editors nor
the author can accept any liability for any consequences arising from the use
thereof, or the information contained therein.

*Many thanks to: Jamie Ambrose for editorial management and design input,
Ian Hughes of Mousemat Design for jacket and text design, Margaret Campbell
of Scan-Hi Digital and Craig Campbell of QSP Print for printing consultancy.
Printed and bound in Scotland by Scotprint.*

contents

For Colin Howell
and
In memory of Sam

I

the truth
about magic

*The ultimate object of magic in all ages
was, and is, to obtain control of
the sources of life.*

W. B. YEATS

To the cynic and those of a scientific turn of mind, the very idea that magic could work would strike them as completely ridiculous. Yet magic is all around us. To our ancient ancestors, the rising of the Sun each morning and its setting in the evening was a magical event. The waxing and waning of the Moon, the coming and going of the seasons in their unending cycle could never be relied upon.

A bad summer meant a poor harvest and starvation in winter. It was essential, therefore, that ancient primitive man took active steps to ensure the return of the life-giving Sun after the winter darkness and cold. This was the dawn of magic.

Our early ancestors were pagan. Long before the advent of Christianity, they worshipped Nature: the things which they could observe. They worshipped the Sun, which gave them warmth and caused their crops to grow, nurtured their animals and encouraged them to reproduce. They worshipped streams and rivers which provided water, trees which shaded them and caves in which they sheltered. They worshipped the Moon, which lit their way at night.

Their deities were Pan, the God of Nature, who ruled the forests and the fields, and the Great Mother, who brought forth new life, protected women in childbirth and nurtured children and animals. These were personified by their priests.

Rituals and petitions were presented to the gods at festivals which celebrated the pagan year. From these events gradually evolved wise men and women who possessed special powers: the ability to foresee events in the lives of the tribe and of individuals, and often to influence these events and cause things to happen for the increase of happiness and well-being – also, sometimes to thwart and frustrate.

By trial and error, these people, who then became known as witches, or 'the wise ones', would devise and develop techniques to work their magic. These techniques became known as spells.

Most people, perhaps in the secret places of their hearts, have a curiosity concerning the old ways. While rationality declares that magic and spells are mere superstition, there is a sustaining desire to believe that, in the distant past, magic did, perhaps, produce results, and that maybe it worked through a natural transmission of events and nothing more.

In the twenty-first century, where science rules and we are surrounded on all sides by technological advances our grandparents could never have envisaged, it takes a degree of faith to acknowledge that magic and spells *can* produce results. The dictionary defines magic as 'the art that by the use of spells supposedly invokes supernatural powers to influence events'. However, magic is more than this. It encompasses the use of herbs, light and incense, but the most powerful ingredient is the human mind – the power of the will: the concentration of human energy directed to the desired result.

A perusal of ancient texts produces spells requiring somewhat grisly ingredients: the heart of a pigeon; a dried, pulverized frog; the legs of a rat. Fortunately, the traditions of magic have made some progress, and modern spells utilize more easily obtained ingredients without losing the essence of essential power.

It is not necessary to embrace pagan beliefs, to become involved with an occult group or to imagine oneself to be a witch in order to work simple spells. All that is required is a measure of faith in one's own ability and an earnest desire to produce results.

One important truth to be borne in mind is that magic itself is neutral; it is neither black nor white. Its base is the power of the mind and the will and the attitude of the operator. Thus, how it affects events lies in the power of the mind and the will and the intention of the operator. Caution must be observed, therefore, and there is always a moral obligation to use magic in moderation and never to try to gain control over another person. The term 'gentle persuasion' should be held in mind.

So we come to the purpose of this book: *Spells to Change Your Life*. During the course of our lives we all encounter situations in which, to some degree, we consider ourselves to be helpless or misused, and we wish that in some small way we could redress the balance and make our presence felt. We do not necessarily wish to hurt or harm anyone, just to feel the satisfaction of responding to injustice and insensitivity.

In truth, it is not white magic, nor is it black magic; rather, it is a shade of pale grey, and it is necessary for the utilizer of these spells to bear this truth in mind.

Practical magic

True practitioners of magic prefer to work outside, with the sounds and ambience of Nature all around them. However, since climatic conditions are not always favourable, it is suggested that, if possible, a room is set aside for the purpose, preferably a room not in constant use – but a bedroom is not a suitable place, since this is an area reserved for rest and relaxation.

The chosen site should always be swept clean and dusted before magical operations. A small table should be utilized for the rituals; this should stand in the centre of the room facing north. On the table should be a free-standing mirror, large enough for the operator to gaze into comfortably from a kneeling position.

It is not necessary to involve oneself in great expense for the ingredients of simple spells. Most of what is required can be purchased from supermarkets, grocery shops, or indeed,

from the bounty of Nature. Herbs, oils, etc., can also be obtained from Magistra, 46 Carlisle Avenue, St Albans, Herts AL3 5LX, tel: +44 (0) 1727 858028; they have a prompt postal service. Alternatively, any magical or herbal supplier should have these things in stock.

Accessories are important from the point of view of concentrating the mind on the task and the result intended. You should remember to obtain your ingredients well before the date on which you intend to work your spell.

The simplest method of charting the phases of the Moon required by the spells is to utilize an *Old Moore's Almanack*, available from most newsagents. The different phases of the Moon for a month are indicated at the bottom of each page. For instance, if a spell is to be worked three days after a New Moon, and the *Almanack* shows that the New Moon is on September 7, the spell should be worked three days later, on September 10.

II

spells for
love & sex

A SPELL TO ATTRACT

Let us suppose that there is a person of the opposite sex to whom you are attracted and there does not seem to exist any obvious signs of reciprocity. You wish to make yourself irresistible to that person. On a practical level, you would obviously be pleasant and agreeable, dress appropriately and be sure that your personal hygiene is above reproach when in that person's company. You should wear your favourite perfume or aftershave always so that your presence is defined by that scent.

On a magical level, to help things along, on the night of a New Moon you should repair to your special room and conduct the spell that follows on page 22.

you will require
- ★ two pink candles
- ★ a charcoal block
- ★ some sweet-smelling incense
- ★ fresh rosemary
- ★ a piece of pink paper
- ★ a length of pink ribbon

Place one candle on each side of the mirror.

In front of the mirror, put the charcoal block in the dish; light the block, blow it into an ember, and sprinkle the incense and a few of the rosemary leaves on it.

Light each candle, and as you do so speak the name of the person you wish to attract. Write your love's name on the piece of pink paper, pass it over the incense and express your desire in words, gazing into the mirror as your do so.

Roll the paper and tie it loosely with a pink ribbon, and then pass it briefly through the candle flames, first left, then right.

You should sleep with the paper placed under your pillow every night until the night of a Full Moon.

TO DISCOVER THE INITIAL OF
A FUTURE HUSBAND OR WIFE

The apple, being sacred to Venus, Goddess of Love, has a long association with divination and magic. An apple cut in half reveals a perfect pentacle, reflecting magic.

Peel an apple in one long strip and let it fall to the ground, where the initial of your future husband or wife will be formed.

To ensure fruition, the peel should be surrounded by a scattering of rosemary and red rose petals and left where it is for three days and three nights.

The peel, petals and rosemary should then be carefully swept up and placed in a small red box or other container, sealed and placed under your bed.

To bring a lover
into your life

This spell should be carried out on the night of a New Moon.

you will require
* two red candles
* a small dish or incense burner
* a charcoal block
* some sweet-smelling incense
* a new, unused pin
* a sprinkling of rose essence
* a picture of yourself
* two half-open red roses
* a small container to hold them

Place one candle each side of the mirror. In front of the mirror, put the charcoal block in the dish; light the block, blow it into an ember. Sprinkle the incense and rose essence on it.

Kneel in front of the altar holding your photograph in open hands, and say three times: 'Queen of Heaven, Star of the Sea, bring my true love here to me.'

Push the pin through the stalks of the roses, about halfway down. Pass them through the incense and place them, joined, in the container.

Douse the candles and leave the joined roses (topped up with water periodically) until the flowers open and then fall.

Collect the petals, place in an unused envelope and sleep with them under your pillow for seven nights.

To rid yourself of an unwanted lover

This is a finality spell and should be carried out immediately after a Full Moon so that it can mature during the waning Moon and reach its zenith of influence during the dark of the Moon.

you will require
* two grey candles
* a small bottle two-thirds full of water
* a cork or screwtop
* a pen
* a small piece of paper
* a photograph of your erstwhile lover, if possible

Place a candle on each side of the mirror, then light them.

Kneel on the floor, holding the photograph, and gaze into the mirror at your own reflection. Verbalize your intent thus: 'I wish that (Name) would leave my life peacefully to find another love.'

Write the person's full name on the paper, fold it several times and place it in the bottle. Screw down the lid, briefly pass the bottle through the flames of the two candles and then place the bottle at the back of the freezing compartment of your fridge and leave undisturbed.

To calm a jealous lover

This spell should be carried out on the night before a Full Moon.

you will require
* two blue candles
* a small dish or incense burner
* a charcoal block
* some sweet-smelling incense
* half a teaspoonful of marjoram
* a photograph of your love
* a few hairs acquired from a pillow or a hairbrush, if possible

Light the charcoal block, blow it into an ember and sprinkle on it the sweet-smelling incense and marjoram.

Place the candles on each side of the mirror and light them.

Place the photograph and hair before you on the altar, close your eyes and cover the photograph with your two hands.

Using your personal energy to calm the situation, imagine the photograph and hair infused with a calming blue light emanating from your hands. Continue to do this for ten minutes.

TO SPICE UP YOUR LOVE LIFE

you will require
* two red candles
* a small dish or incense burner
* a charcoal block
* some sweet-smelling incense
* vanilla essence
* a photograph of your lover and yourself
* some red pepper
* two pieces of red ribbon

Light the charcoal block, blow it into an ember and sprinkle on it the sweet-smelling incense. Place one candle on each side of the mirror and light them. Into the incense, sprinkle a few drops of vanilla essence.

Place the photographs face to face, and on them sprinkle some red pepper. On top of this lay two pieces of red ribbon in the sign of an 'x'. Then wait for the fireworks!

To strengthen a
love relationship

This spell should be carried out on the night of a Friday nearest the New Moon.

you will require
- ✳ two pink candles
- ✳ a charcoal block
- ✳ a small dish or incense burner
- ✳ some sweet-smelling incense
- ✳ rose essence
- ✳ three pieces of red ribbon
  12 inches in length
- ✳ a lock of your hair and some of your lover's
- ✳ a length of common ivy plant

Light the charcoal block, blow it into an ember and sprinkle on it the sweet-smelling incense and rose essence.

Place the candles on each side of the mirror and light them.

Kneel before the altar, tie a knot at one end of the three pieces of ribbon and make a plait of the ribbons, incorporating into the plait both your own hair and that of your lover.

As you do this, gaze into the mirror and say, 'As our hair is wound in close, may our love be in repose.'

Lay the plait on the altar and surround it in a circle with the wreath of ivy. Douse the candles and leave the plait on the altar for seven days and nights.

TO SWEETEN A LOVE AFFAIR NOT RUNNING SMOOTHLY

you will require
* two pink candles, one on each side of the mirror
* two small pieces of paper and a small receptacle capable of holding them without folding them
* some honey

Light the candles. Write the name of your lover on a small piece of paper, and on another, your own name. Place the paper that contains your own name over the paper containing your lover's name so that the two names touch.

Pour some honey in the container so that it covers the papers. Douse the candles. Leave the container on the altar for three days and three nights. Remove the container and place it at the back of a cupboard.

TO REMOVE A RIVAL IN
A LOVE AFFAIR

This spell should be carried out on the night after a Full Moon. No candles or incense are required in this instance.

Write the name of your rival on a piece of paper. Place the paper, folded, in a small bottle. Fill the bottle with earth and bury it in the garden at midnight.

Over the area where the bottle is buried, scatter a few leaves from an ash tree.

TO BRING BACK A LOVER

This spell is intended to heal a breach in a relationship that follows a lovers' quarrel. Continual quarrels often indicate a lack of commitment, and there should be an awareness that sometimes it is better to 'let go'.

This spell should be carried out on a Friday nearest a Full Moon.

you will require
* two new blue candles
* a charcoal block
* a small dish or incense burner
* some sweet-smelling incense
* fresh rosemary
* a photograph of your lover
* a piece of red ribbon, about
  12 inches long

Score your lover's full name on the candles with any pointed instrument. Place the lighted

candles before the mirror so that their light is reflected. Light the charcoal block, blow it into an ember, and sprinkle on some sweet incense, then add a few rosemary leaves.

Place the photograph of your lover before you on the altar. Carefully weave the piece of red ribbon tightly around your right index finger, and rest this finger on the photograph for about five minutes while you visualize your lover returning to you.

Allow the ribbon to unravel over the photo while you speak your wish: '(Name) return to me. I want only you and my love is true.'

The ribbon should be left on the photograph until the night of a Full Moon. The candles should be allowed to burn to half their length, and then be extinguished.

A SPELL OF ASSERTION

If your lover is playing fast and loose with you and you feel no sense of security in the relationship, this spell will cause him or her to reflect and begin to appreciate you and your qualities.

This spell should be carried out on a Monday evening nearest to a New Moon.

you will require
  * two brown candles, one on each side of the mirror
  * a charcoal block
  * a small dish or incense burner
  * some sweet-smelling incense
  * a small photograph of your lover
  * a handful of oak leaves
  * some rue
  * a length of brown ribbon

Light the candles. Place the photograph of your lover on the altar; cover it with the oak leaves. Light the charcoal block, blow it into an ember and sprinkle on some sweet incense followed by a small amount of the rue. As you do so, say aloud, looking into the mirror: 'As I use the strength of oak, may new life my love invoke.'

Place your right hand over the photograph and for a few minutes meditate on a renewal of confidence in the relationship.

Extinguish the candles and then leave the photograph on the altar for three days and three nights.

Place the photograph and some of the oak leaves in a small box, tie it with brown ribbon and bury it at the foot of an oak tree.

A SPELL TO AID CONCEPTION

This simple spell sets the scene to aid conception and should be carried out on the night of a New Moon.

For a girl child, you should use one pink candle, for a boy child, a blue candle. A clean white cloth should be placed on the altar and the candle placed before the centre of the mirror so that its light is reflected.

you will require
  * a small dish or incense burner containing a burning charcoal block
  * some sweet-smelling incense
  * a bay leaf
  * a sprinkling of sage
  * a teaspoon of honey
  * a cotton handkerchief, freshly laundered
  * a piece of clean, white paper
  * a small amount of plasticine in either pink or blue, according to the sex preferred

Kneel before the altar. Light the candle, sprinkle the incense on the charcoal block and then mould the plasticine into the shape of a male or female child.

Lay the figure on the altar on the piece of paper and, dipping your finger into the honey, anoint the figure of the baby, front and back. Sprinkle the sage on the incense and place the bay leaf on the figure.

Take the figure in your hands and, gazing into the mirror, say three times, 'This is the child I wish to conceive. May my wish be granted.' Meditate on your wish for a few minutes, still gazing into the mirror.

Leave the figure on the altar before the burning candle for one hour. Wrap it in the cotton handkerchief and place it under your pillow each night until the night of the Full Moon.

III

spells for
family & friendship

BLESSING FOR A NEW BABY

This spell should be carried out on the night of a New Moon.

you will require
- ⋆ two yellow candles
- ⋆ a small dish or incense burner
- ⋆ a charcoal block
- ⋆ some sweet-smelling incense
- ⋆ a picture of the baby
- ⋆ the Sun card from a Tarot deck since the Sun is appropriate for a child's blessing
- ⋆ rose oil
- ⋆ a few red rose petals

Light the charcoal block, blow it into an ember and sprinkle on some sweet incense and a few drops of rose oil. Place the candles on each side of the mirror and light them.

Place the baby's photograph on the altar surrounded by the rose petals. Place the Sun card so that it covers the photograph of the child.

Close your eyes and hold your hands over the photograph and Tarot card, summoning positive, loving thoughts, and say: 'Child of light, child of love, blessings to you from above. Sun to greet your every day, peace and radiance bless your way.'

Pass the photo through the candle flames: first left, then right. Cover the photograph with the rose petals and leave on the altar for seven days and seven nights.

FOR GOOD HEALTH
IN YOUR CHILD

This spell should be worked on a Sunday evening nearest to a New Moon.

you will require
* two green candles
* a small dish or incense burner
* a charcoal block
* some sweet-smelling incense
* a photograph of the child
* a handful of fresh oak leaves
* five plain green beads
* a large needle
* thick thread to string the beads

Light the charcoal block, blow it into an ember, and sprinkle on some sweet incense.

Light the candles. Place the child's photograph in the centre of the altar in front of the mirror.

Place the oak leaves in a circle around the photograph. Hold each bead in turn in the centre of your palm and spiritually impregnate it with your thoughts for health and protection, alternately.

Thread the needle and draw each bead onto the thread, concentrating your desire on each bead in turn. Secure them all at the end with five knots.

Place the beads over the photograph and say: 'May my child (Name) flourish and grow as strong as the oak tree and in perfect health all the days of his/her life.'

Leave on the altar for five days and five nights, then hang the beads on a corner of the child's cot or bed or under the mattress.

TO ENSURE A CONTENTED
AND HAPPY CHILD

This spell should be worked seven nights after a New Moon.

you will require
* two yellow candles
* a small dish or incense burner
* a charcoal block
* some sweet-smelling incense
* seven gold-coloured beads
* a large needle
* thread to string the beads
* a photograph of the child
* a little turmeric powder
* a few yellow primroses, cowslips or buttercups

Light the charcoal block and blow it into an ember. Light the candles and place the child's photograph in the centre of the altar before the mirror.

Scatter sweet incense on the smouldering charcoal block and sprinkle the turmeric on top. Place the yellow flower petals around the photograph. On the photo itself, rest the seven beads: six in a circle, one in the centre.

Place the palms of your hands over the photograph and beads and for about five minutes; imagine them being infused with a golden light from your hands.

Thread the needle and, taking up each bead in turn, mentally consecrate it with a desired quality – *i.e.* happiness, contentment, a sunny nature, a good digestion, an even temperament, peaceful sleeping, playfulness.

Secure each bead with one knot; after the last bead, secure with seven knots and place them on the photograph saying, 'May angelic beings protect this child and bless him/her with peace and joy.'

Repeat six times. Leave the beads on the photograph until the candles have burned down, then hang them on a corner of the cot or bed, or place under the mattress.

To soothe a grieving heart

For someone who is depressed and unhappy through grief or misfortune, this spell will lift their spirits and heal their hearts. It should be carried out on the seventh night after a New Moon.

you will require
* a clean, white cloth to cover the altar
* a vase containing fresh white flowers
* two bright-yellow candles
* a small dish or incense burner
* a charcoal block
* some sweet-smelling incense
* a photograph of the person concerned
* 24 inches of yellow ribbon
* a few leaves of basil, known for its calming effect
* six pansies, otherwise known as 'heartsease'

for the casting

Light the charcoal block, blow it into an ember, and sprinkle on some sweet incense to attract good influences. Cover the altar with the clean, white cloth and set out the vase containing fresh, white flowers.

Kneel before the altar in a relaxed mental and emotional attitude of love and compassion. Light the candles and place them on each side of the mirror.

Look first into the mirror at your reflection, and then concentrate your gaze on the photograph before saying aloud: 'I cover you with light and joy as I bind you with the Sun. May tears and sorrow disappear and heartache all be gone.'

Take the yellow ribbon, bind it around the index finger of your right hand and hold this finger to the centre of your forehead: the area of the psychic 'third eye'. Blow a soft breath onto the photograph, saying, as you do so, *Hu*. Breath is the power of life, and you are sending renewed life to your friend or relative.

Release the ribbon and let it fall and cover the photograph. Place the pansies on the photograph, then place two leaves of basil on the incense and the remainder on the photograph, repeating the spell as you do so.

Leave the photo on the altar undisturbed for seven days and seven nights.

Blessing for an animal which has died

The loss of an animal friend through age, illness or accident is always heart-rending, but if we can assume that they survive death, we shall be reunited eventually.

Animals often stay for a time in their old home, and people with psychic vision will be aware of their presence. A simple blessing will help them on their way. It can be carried out in the evening of any waxing Moon.

you will require
* a blue candle
* a small dish or incense burner
* a charcoal block
* some sweet-smelling incense
* rosemary essence
* a photograph of the two of you
* a knife with a sharp point

Light the charcoal block and blow it into an ember. Sprinkle sweet incense on it, and place the photograph on the altar.

With the knife, carve the name of the animal on the candle and then anoint it with rosemary essence. Light the candle and place it before the mirror so that its light is reflected.

Kneel before the altar, holding (if possible) a favourite toy of your pet, and say, 'I give thanks to the gods for the love and the life of my animal friend (Name). May the Lord and Lady of all creatures receive him/her own kind into their kingdom where he/she may find peace and happiness with his/her own kind.'

The toy should be buried in the earth.

To smooth over a personality clash and prevent arguing

This simple spell will help ease relationships. It should be carried out on the night following a New Moon.

you will require
* two green candles
* a small dish or incense burner
* a charcoal block
* some sweet-smelling incense
* a small, shallow glass dish
* a green ink pen
* a piece of parchment paper
* some oil of ginger and oil of cloves: the former to induce warmth, the latter to assist in friendly debate
* photographs of the warring parties (If these are not available, use their names and dates of birth.)

Light the charcoal block and blow it into an ember. Sprinkle sweet incense on it.

Light the candles, placing one on each side of the mirror. Write the names and birth dates of the warring parties on the parchment paper in green ink. Place the photographs, if available, on each side of the glass dish.

Place the parchment paper inside the dish and sprinkle liberally with the oil of ginger and oil of cloves while you say: 'May peace prevail and friendship rule. All quarrels end and joy ensue.'

Leave the altar untouched for three days and three nights.

TO AVOID A DIVORCE

This spell should be carried out seven days after a New Moon.

you will require
- ✳ two red candles
- ✳ a small dish or incense burner
- ✳ a charcoal block
- ✳ some lavender essence
- ✳ a few red rose petals
- ✳ a perfect red apple, preferably plucked from a tree (but a firm, bought one will suffice)
- ✳ two very small pieces of parchment
- ✳ two long, new pins
- ✳ a red pen
- ✳ a small knife
- ✳ a teaspoonful of frankincense

Light the charcoal block; blow it into an ember. Light the candles; place one on each side of the mirror. On the smouldering charcoal block, sprinkle the frankincense and a few drops of lavender essence. Carefully cut the apple in half.

On each of the pieces of parchment, write both full names of the married couple and place them between the two halves of the apple, saying: 'As the apple is sacred to the Goddess of Love, may these two people be renewed on Earth and above.'

Place the two halves together and secure with the pins diagonally. Leave the apple on the altar for 24 hours, surrounded with the rose petals.

Afterwards, bake the apple in an oven until it looks whole. Invite the couple for a meal and place a little of the apple in the food they eat.

To smooth divorce

When divorce is inevitable, this spell can be worked to smooth proceedings and to help allow the couple to accept the situation without rancour or bitterness.

The spell should be worked three nights after a New Moon.

you will require

* two blue candles
* a small dish or incense burner
* a charcoal block
* some sweet-smelling incense
* a blue pen
* a knife with a sharp tip
* a ruler
* two pieces of blue paper 6 inches x 4 inches
* a small photograph of each person, preferably passport-size
* two marigold flowers
* some lavender flowers
* two 6-inch lengths of narrow blue ribbon

for the casting

Light the charcoal block and blow it into an
ember. Kneel before the altar and scatter some
sweet incense on it.

On each candle, engrave with the pointed knife
the names of the divorcing couple: the male on
the left, the female on the right.

Light the candles and place on either side of the
altar. Place each photograph separately in the
centre of the pieces of paper.

With the ruler, draw a square around each
photograph, then another outside this, and yet
another so that each photograph is contained
within three squares.

Hold your hands, palms downward on each
photograph – left hand over the male, right
hand over the female – and meditate on them

for a few minutes, imagining each surrounded by a blue light. Then say aloud three times: 'Flower of light, flower of peace, blossom in the hearts of these two people, renewing life and hope in the future.'

Sprinkle the marigold petals and lavender flowers over the photographs. Roll each one separately and secure by winding a piece of blue ribbon around them, each secured by three knots.

Leave them undisturbed on the altar for three days and three nights, then place separately in two drawers which are seldom opened.

Allow the candles to burn down over the engraved names, and then throw them in running water three days apart.

To soothe and
heal family feuds

This spell should be carried out nine nights after a New Moon.

you will require
* a black candle
* some rosemary oil
* a piece of parchment paper
* a black pen
* a yard of black ribbon
* scissors
* a fairly large flameproof dish

Place the candle in the centre of the mirror and before lighting it, anoint it with the rosemary oil.

On the paper write a list of all the family aggravations and factions to be solved.

Cut the black ribbon into small pieces, each one representing a problem.

Concentrate your mind on each problem in turn, clearly and decisively, then take the paper, hold it in the candle flame until it burns, saying: 'May peace and goodwill reign and rule, care and love be the tool. Spite and envy leave our lives; joy and happiness now will thrive.'

Place the burning paper in the flameproof dish, and to the flames add the separate pieces of ribbon.

Allow the candle to burn down and bury the remainder in earth, then cast the ashes of paper and ribbon to the four winds.

TO DRAW CHILDREN IN
A FAMILY CLOSER

This spell should be worked seven nights after
a New Moon.

you will require
* two pink candles
* a small dish or incense burner
* a charcoal block
* some sweet-smelling incense
* as many bay leaves as there are children
* essence of rose
* photographs of the children concerned
* a yard of pink ribbon

Light the charcoal block in the dish and blow it
into an ember. Place one candle on each side of
the mirror. Before lighting them, anoint each
with rose oil, intoning the full names of the
children as you do so.

On the smouldering charcoal block, sprinkle some sweet incense and a few drops of the rose essence.

Place the photographs of the children on the altar, hold the palms of your hands over them and say: 'All the good spirits guard and guide, and love be ever at your side. Draw you close each to the other; bond you each as to your mother.'

Roll the photographs one inside the other with a bay leaf between each and secure with the pink ribbon.

Leave on the altar for seven days and seven nights, then place at the back of a drawer which is seldom opened.

A SPELL FOR FAMILY PROSPERITY

This spell should be worked seven nights after a Full Moon.

you will require
* two gold candles, on either side of the altar
* seven walnuts
* seven five-penny pieces
* seven whole cloves
* seven bay leaves
* some gold foil

Open the walnuts carefully; clean out the shells. In each shell, place a five-penny piece, a clove and a bay leaf. Glue the two halves of each shell and fold gold foil around them. Place them on a window sill so that the Full Moon shines on them, then cover them with a sheet of gold foil until the night of the next Full Moon.

A CHARM TO PROTECT YOUR HOME

This spell should be worked on the night of a New Moon.

you will require
* a small green glass bottle with a screw lid
* honey
* crushed garlic
* some of your own nail parings
* a length of narrow green ribbon

Half-fill the bottle with honey and add some crushed garlic. On top, place a few of your nail parings.

Seal the bottle, and tie around it a narrow green ribbon.

Secrete the bottle in a place where it will not be seen near the front door of your home.

To have an object returned

This spell should be carried out three nights after a New Moon.

you will require
* two grey candles
* a small dish or incense burner
* a charcoal block
* some sweet-smelling incense
* a sprig of rosemary
* a fresh rose of any colour
* a red pen
* a piece of parchment paper
* a new nail

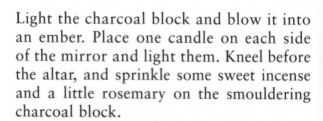

Light the charcoal block and blow it into an ember. Place one candle on each side of the mirror and light them. Kneel before the altar, and sprinkle some sweet incense and a little rosemary on the smouldering charcoal block.

On the parchment paper, write the name of the person who possesses the article you wish returned. Next to the name, make a simple drawing of the object and describe it underneath, *i.e.* book, pen, etc.

Close your eyes and hold the palms of your hands over the parchment paper. Concentrate on the person and the article and imagine it being returned. Do this for five minutes.

Place the nail on the paper pointing north, south, east or west in whichever direction the person lives. On top of the nail place the rose.

Allow the candles to burn down fully and leave the objects on the altar for three days and three nights, then roll them together and put at the back of a drawer seldom opened. When the article is returned, bury the nail in earth.

To seek good relations with in-laws or a lover's family

This spell should be carried out on the night of a New Moon.

you will require
* two pink candles
* a small dish or incense burner
* a charcoal block
* some sweet-smelling incense
* some vanilla oil
* a teaspoonful of sweet basil
* a photograph of the family concerned, or their full names written with red ink on a piece of white parchment paper

Place one candle on either side of the mirror. Light the candles and, carefully, while they are alight, anoint them with the vanilla oil. As you do so, recite the names

of all the people with whom you wish to achieve harmony.

Light the charcoal block and blow it into an ember. When it smoulders, add sweet incense and one-quarter of the teaspoonful of sweet basil.

Spread the palms of your hands over the photograph or written names and concentrate thoughts of peace and amity for about five minutes, then speak aloud these words five times: 'May light and peace embrace us.'

Sprinkle the remaining sweet basil on the photograph or names and leave undisturbed for five days and five nights.

TO DEAL WITH AN INTERFERING IN-LAW

This spell should be carried out two nights before a Full Moon to give power to the spell and then allow a decline.

you will require

* a photograph of the person, full-length and alone
* a small dish or incense burner
* a charcoal block
* some sweet-smelling incense
* a red cord 12 inches in length
* one grey candle placed before the mirror so that its light is reflected
* a small amount of the resin Dragon's Blood, in powder form
* a pair of scissors
* a small piece of sticking plaster
* a new pin

for the casting

Light the charcoal block and blow it into an ember.

Kneel before the altar with the photograph before you. Gaze into the mirror and mentally imagine a peaceful, tranquil period without interference in your life.

Onto the burning charcoal block, sprinkle some sweet-smelling incense, then immediately a small amount of Dragon's Blood.

Place your hands on the photograph and say three times: 'As I bind you mouth and limb, it is with love, not evil whim.'

With the scissors, cut a tiny piece of the sticking plaster and place over the mouth on the photograph, then roll the photograph and secure it from top to bottom with the red cord. Secure the cord by pushing the pin through it and the photograph.

Sprinkle a further amount of Dragon's Blood on the incense, hold the rolled photograph and repeat the incantation twice more.

The photograph should be left on the altar until the night of the next New Moon, by which time the magic should have become effective.

To win friends and influence people

This spell should be carried out on the night a Full Moon.

you will require
- two pink candles, one on each side of the mirror
- a bowl of water, standing in the centre of the altar
- red rose petals
- essence of rose
- a joss stick
- a photograph of yourself with friends

Light the candles. In the bowl, sprinkle some red rose petals and a few drops of essence of rose. Instead of incense, a joss stick with the fragrance of rose should be lit.

The photograph of yourself with friends should be on the altar.

Kneel before the altar, hold the photograph in your hands, and gaze into the mirror, imagining yourself surrounded by happy faces as you do so.

Hold this image and say aloud: 'Power of friendship, come to me, bringing joy and hilarity.' Repeat three times and then, still kneeling before the altar, meditate quietly on your desire for a while.

Place the photograph on the bowl of water and rose petals and leave it there for nine days and nine nights.

A CHARM TO ATTRACT FRIENDS

you will require

* two pink candles
* a small dish or incense burner
* a charcoal block
* some sweet-smelling incense
* a lodestone for its magnetic qualities
* a turquoise stone to enhance communication and friendship
* a photograph of yourself
* a hematite stone, for optimistic inspiration
* some rose oil
* 2 oz of pink rosebuds
* a knife with a sharp point
* a small nutmeg, for attraction
* a small pink bag with a drawstring

Place one candle on either side of the mirror. Place your photograph in the centre of the altar and then with the knife, inscribe your name on each of the candles.

Light the candles, and with the rose oil, carefully anoint them, slowly concentrating on your desire for friends as you do so.

Light the charcoal block and blow it into an ember. Sprinkle with the incense.

Place the stones, the rosebuds and the nutmeg on your photograph and leave undisturbed for one hour, allowing the candles to continue burning. At the end of this time, take each of the stones in your hand, concentrating on your desire, and place them in the bag, followed by the nutmeg and the rosebuds.

Close the drawstring, pass the bag briefly through first the left candle, then the right and finally through the incense. The bag should be carried with you at all times, and at night placed under your pillow.

TO HELP A FRIEND IN NEED

This charm is for unspecified problems and is calculated to bring about a change of circumstances more beneficial to the subject's life. It should be carried out two nights after a New Moon.

you will require

* two red candles
* a small dish or incense burner
* a charcoal block
* some sweet-smelling incense
* a sodalite stone, which has qualities of balance between mind and body
* a tiger's eye stone, to promote bravery, perception and insight
* a few slippery elm leaves or bark, for protection
* five stalks of fresh rosemary, to produce sharpness of mind
* a small dark-red drawstring bag, to hold the articles
* a photograph of your friend

for the casting

Light the charcoal block and blow it into an ember.

Light the candles and place them on each side of the mirror. Scatter sweet incense on the smouldering charcoal block.

The photograph of your friend should be propped up facing the mirror so that it is reflected. The stones and leaves should be placed in a circle around the photograph. With the candles still burning, leave everything undisturbed for one hour.

At the end of the hour, carefully place the stones and leaves in the red bag and pull the drawstring closed.

Lay the photograph flat on the altar and put the bag on top. Hold your hands over the bag and say: 'Lords of light and powers of peace, embrace this life and tumult cease. Surround (Name) with help and aid, and may all sorrow and suffering fade.' Repeat once.

The bag should be passed briefly through each candle flame – left then right – and through the incense.

Leave the bag on the altar on top of the photograph for two days and two nights, and then hand it to your friend, advising that it should be kept with him or her at all times.

To assist in a long and happy friendship

This spell should be carried out on a Friday evening nearest to a New Moon.

you will require
* two green candles
* a small dish or incense burner
* a charcoal block
* some sweet-smelling incense
* a little powdered nutmeg
* a few drops of rose oil
* a sprig of rosemary
* a piece of parchment paper
* a green pen
* a 12-inch length of narrow green ribbon
* a photograph of your friend, if possible

Light the charcoal block in the dish and blow it into an ember.

Before lighting the candles and placing them on each side of the mirror, write with the point of the pen the full name of your friend on each candle and anoint each with the rose oil.

Onto the smouldering charcoal block, add a little sweet incense and a few drops of rose oil.

Place the photograph on the altar. On the parchment paper write the name of your friend. Hold the palms of your hands over the two and say: 'Herbs and candles, work my will; love and friendship, my life fill.'

Place the sprig of rosemary on the photo and parchment paper and roll it, securing it with the green ribbon. Leave this on the altar until the following Friday evening, and then place in a bottom drawer.

To heal a rift between friends

This spell should be worked two nights after a New Moon.

you will require
* two pink candles
* a small photograph of each of the friends
* some lavender flowers, to engender calmness and peace
* a red pen
* a piece of parchment paper, 2 inches x 4 inches
* an amethyst stone, to incorporate healing and divine love
* a knife with a sharp point

Before lighting the candles, with the point of the knife, inscribe on each candle the names of the two estranged friends.

Light the candles and, in the centre of the altar before the mirror, place the piece of parchment paper, and on top of that, the small photographs.

With the pen, draw a circle around the two photographs. Between them place the amethyst and sprinkle the lavender flowers over both the photographs.

Place the palms of your hands over the photographs and say aloud, 'May these two friends (Names) be reconciled in love and equanimity and exist believing in the equality of all that lives.' Repeat the words once.

Allow the candles to burn for two hours, leaving the articles on the altar for two days and two nights.

A BLESSING OF FORGIVENESS

If you have encountered the pain of betrayal and wish to be relieved of this, you should carry out this ritual on the night of a New Moon.

you will require
* a blue candle
* a small dish or incense burner
* a charcoal block
* some sweet-smelling incense
* a photograph of your erstwhile friend
* a few pansies (or essence of the same)

Light the charcoal block and blow it into an ember, then scatter sweet incense and add the pansies (also known as heartsease) or a few drops of the essence.

Light the candle and place it before the mirror so that its light is reflected. Place the photograph in front of the candle.

Hold the palms of your hands over the photograph and remember in your mind the pain of the hurt; then imagine it crumbling and drifting away and say: 'Comforter of souls, healer of hearts, restore peace and concord between myself and (Name), as I forgive him/her for the pain of offence. May all sorrow be melted in the balm of tranquillity.'

Leave the photograph on the altar for 24 hours, then place it in a drawer which is seldom opened.

To deal with
a noisy neighbour

This spell, called Four Thieves Vinegar, is to quieten a noisy neighbour and encourage him/her to move. The spell should be carried out on the night of a Full Moon.

you will require
  * one black candle
  * a small dish or incense burner
  * a charcoal block
  * a small piece of parchment paper
  * a bottle almost filled with garlic cloves and covered with wine vinegar
  * a cap for the bottle
  * some cedar oil
  * a black pen

Light the charcoal block and blow it into an ember. Light the candle.

Kneel before the altar. Place the candle before the centre of the mirror, so that its light is reflected.

Sprinkle a few drops of the cedar oil on the smouldering charcoal block, then write the name of your noisy neighbour on the parchment paper.

Hold the paper in your hands, gaze into the mirror, and say: 'I wish this person quietness and peace and to leave my life in tranquillity.'

Fold the paper and place it in the bottle, screw down the lid and pass the bottle through the flame of the candle. The same night that you do the spell, throw the bottle into a fast-flowing river.

IV

spells for
the workplace

TO COUNTER UNPLEASANTNESS
IN THE WORKPLACE

If you are troubled in your working environment by a bullying and unpleasant person, this spell will relieve the situation.

you will require
- ∗ one black and one white candle
- ∗ a small dish or incense burner
- ∗ a charcoal block
- ∗ a little Dragon's Blood
- ∗ a black pen
- ∗ a piece of white parchment paper
- ∗ a ruler
- ∗ 6 inches of narrow black ribbon

Light the charcoal block; blow it into an ember. Light the candles. On the smouldering charcoal block, sprinkle a little Dragon's Blood.

Write the full name of your tormentor on the paper, and next to it a rough drawing of a face with an exaggerated mouth which you then cover with the pen in firm strokes.

Around the two, using the ruler, draw two squares, one inside the other, blocking the paths of that person. Sprinkle Dragon's Blood on the square, then carefully roll it up and secure it with the black ribbon.

Silently pass the rolled parchment through first the black candle and then the white.

The same night, bury the parchment in the earth and sprinkle the remaining Dragon's Blood over the top.

TO CHANGE A DEPRESSED
AND DARK MOOD

If you find yourself in a depressed state of mind
or a dark mood due to work-related matters,
work this spell on the night of a New Moon.

you will require
* two blue candles
* a small dish or incense burner
* a charcoal block
* some sweet-smelling incense
* half a teaspoonful of grated garlic
* some lavender oil
* two small bowls containing water

Light the charcoal block; blow it into an ember.
Anoint the candles with the lavender oil,
slowly and deliberately, holding in your mind
the circumstances which are depressing you.
Light the candles and sprinkle some incense
on the smouldering charcoal block.

Kneel before the altar, take one of the bowls in your hands and look deeply into it. Speak aloud all the dark, depressing thoughts that arise in your mind and project them into the water.

When you have finished, sprinkle the garlic on top of the water. Then take into your hands the other bowl and in the same way, thank the gods for all the blessings in your life, enumerating them one by one.

When you have finished, drink some of the water and on the remainder pour a few drops of lavender water. Leave it on the altar undisturbed for two days and two nights. The bowl containing the garlic should be poured outside into the Earth with words of thanks to Mother Earth for absorbing your dark mood.

TO BE SUCCESSFUL IN
BUSINESS UNDERTAKINGS

This spell should be carried out four days after a New Moon.

you will require
* two green candles
* a small dish or incense burner
* a charcoal block
* some sweet-smelling incense
* a horse chestnut
* some eucalyptus oil
* fresh thyme leaves
* a photograph of yourself
* a knife with a point
* a small bowl of water

Light the charcoal block and blow it into an ember. Anoint the candles slowly with the eucalyptus oil. If you have a particular business deal in mind, think of this while you are anointing; otherwise, concentrate on general business success.

Light the candles. On the smouldering charcoal block, sprinkle some sweet incense and a few fresh thyme leaves.

With the tip of the knife, carve your name into the horse chestnut. Pass it over the photograph and say: 'Success in business close to me, may I work with integrity.' Repeat this spell four times, then blow your breath slowly over the horse chestnut, imagining your power being absorbed before placing it into the bowl of water.

Sprinkle some fresh thyme on the water. Stand the bowl on your photograph. Leave it undisturbed for four days and four nights.

To be successful in getting a particular job

This spell should be worked on the night of a New Moon.

you will require
* two purple candles
* a small dish or incense burner
* a charcoal block
* some sweet-smelling incense
* a pointed knife
* purple ink
* a photograph of yourself
* a piece of lapis lazuli stone
* two sprigs of fresh rosemary
* a fresh egg
* a letter indicating an interview or other connection with the position you are seeking

Light the charcoal block and blow it into an ember. Sprinkle some sweet incense and a few rosemary leaves onto the smouldering charcoal block.

On one candle, scratch your name with the knife, and on the other candle the name of the prospective employer.

Light the candles; the one etched with your name should be on the right of the mirror.

Place the letter on the altar with your photograph in the centre, and in the centre of the photograph put the lapis lazuli. Sprinkle some rosemary leaves in a circle around your photograph and the lapis lazuli.

Take the egg and the pen and cover the whole surface with your name alternating with the name of the firm involved, concentrating on your desire.

Place the egg next to the stone, close your eyes and for as long as you can maintain it, at least 15 minutes, hold your hands over the articles and say aloud, 'I will be successful in getting this job.'

This invocation should be repeated for a further two nights. The articles should be left undisturbed for a further seven days and nights.

When you learn that you have been successful, bury the egg whole and without breaking it in a shallow hole in the earth.

To deal with an unfair boss

This spell should be worked four nights after a New Moon.

you will require
- two blue candles
- a small dish or incense burner
- a charcoal block
- some sweet-smelling incense
- a blue-nibbed pen
- a sharp-tipped knife
- a few drops of lavender oil
- a few drops of geranium oil
- a piece of white paper 4 inches square
- a 6-inch length of narrow blue ribbon
- a sprig of fresh lavender

for the casting

Light the charcoal block and blow it into an ember.

On one of the candles, etch your name with the knife, on the other the name of the offending person.

Anoint the candles with the lavender oil and as you do so, concentrate on the unfairness and imagine it being wiped away.

Light the candles, placing the one with your name on it to the right of the mirror. Sprinkle sweet incense on the smouldering charcoal block and add a few drops of geranium oil.

On the paper, write the name of your unfair superior and roughly draw around it two squares, one inside the other. Hold your hands over the paper, close your eyes and concentrate on your superior, bringing an awareness of the unfairness, saying four times: 'Peace and fairness cede this spell: in the workplace make all things well.'

Finally, sprinkle the fresh lavender on the paper, roll it up and secure it with the ribbon, tying the ends with four knots.

Lay it on the altar and sprinkle it with lavender and geranium oil. Leave undisturbed for four days and four nights.

To get a rise in salary

This spell should be worked on the third night after a New Moon.

you will require
* one gold and one silver candle
* a small dish or incense burner
* a charcoal block
* some sweet-smelling incense
* a sharp knife
* a silver-nibbed pen
* a small piece of white paper
* a photograph of yourself
* a three-foot length each of narrow green, royal blue and metallic gold ribbon
* nine whole cloves
* 12 silver coins

Light the charcoal block and blow it into an ember.

With the knife, etch your name on the silver candle, and on the gold candle the name of your employer. Light the candles and place the gold one on the left side of the mirror.

Sprinkle some of the sweet incense onto the smouldering charcoal block, and in the centre of it, place three of the cloves.

On the piece of paper, write the name of the firm or your employer and place this in the centre of the altar on top of your photograph. Place the nine cloves at equal intervals around them.

Tie the three ribbons at one end with three knots and begin to braid or plait them. With each turn, imagine vividly an increased salary cheque.

When you have finished braiding the ribbons, secure them with three knots.

Finally, take the two knotted ends and tie them together with three more knots, forming a circle. Place this on top of your photograph and sprinkle around and inside it the 12 silver coins.

Leave the items undisturbed on the altar for three days and three nights.

CANDLE SPELL TO OBTAIN A WISH

This spell should be carried out two nights after a New Moon.

you will require
* five candles of the colour symbolizing your wish

Choose red candles for love, sex and passion; green candles for health; orange for energy; yellow for confidence, attraction or persuasion; blue for success, fertility or good luck.

Light the candles and concentrate deeply on your wish, passing your gaze continually from one candle to the other in order. Allow the candles to burn down halfway.

The ritual can be carried out on the next evening and the candles allowed to burn down.

V

spells for
luck & prosperity

A CHARM TO PROMOTE LUCK

This ritual should be carried out on the night of the New Moon.

you will require
- ✴ two gold candles
- ✴ a small dish or incense burner
- ✴ a charcoal block
- ✴ some sweet-smelling incense
- ✴ a bay leaf
- ✴ a few flowers and leaves of St John's Wort
- ✴ a few leaves of rue
- ✴ essence of vervain
- ✴ a lodestone, the stone of magnetism
- ✴ a small photograph of the person for whom the charm is being prepared
- ✴ three gold beads
- ✴ a green drawstring bag

Light the charcoal block and blow it into an ember. Light the candles and scatter sweet

incense on the smouldering charcoal block. Lay the photograph in the centre of the altar; on it place the three gold beads. Pour a few drops of the essence of vervain on the incense and place the herbs around the photograph.

Hold the palms of your hand over the photo and say: 'Powers of luck and prosperity, Three special wishes sent to thee: grant good fortune, happy life and peaceful health.' Take up each gold bead in turn, hold it in the palms of your hands and repeat the verse over each bead; afterwards, place the bead in the bag. Add the herbs and the lodestone and close with the drawstring.

Pass the bag briefly and quickly through the left candle, then the right and finally through the smoke of the incense. The bag should be carried in a handbag or pocket at all times.

A CHARM TO ATTRACT MONEY

This ritual should be carried out two nights before a Full Moon.

you will require
- ✳ two silver candles
- ✳ a small dish or incense burner
- ✳ a charcoal block
- ✳ some sweet-smelling incense
- ✳ five silver coins
- ✳ a bloodstone, to attract money
- ✳ an amazonite stone, to attract success
- ✳ a red drawstring bag
- ✳ some poppy seeds, for bounty
- ✳ a few leaves of rue
- ✳ a nutmeg
- ✳ essence of vervain, to reflect wealth
- ✳ a few seeds of the flower honesty, representing the Moon's beneficent aspect

Light the charcoal block and blow it into an ember. Light the candles and scatter sweet incense on the smouldering charcoal block. Add a few drops of essence of vervain.

Before the mirror place the silver coins and cover them with the herbs and nutmeg. The poppy seeds should be placed in a small dish.

Leave the articles before the mirror on the altar for one hour with the candles burning. Then, take up each coin in turn, hold it in the palm of your hand and say, 'Power of money come to me, honestly, to make me free.' Repeat with each coin and place in the bag. Finally, add the stones and the herbs and close the bag with the drawstring.

Place the bag in the light of the Moon for two nights. Then, carry in a pocket or handbag.

To obtain a
special wish

This spell should be worked three nights after a New Moon.

you will require
* two red candles
* a crystal resting on a piece of black velvet
* rose oil
* a few red rose petals

Before lighting the candles, anoint each slowly with the rose oil, voicing your wish firmly as you do so.

Gaze into the crystal, thinking of your wish and willing power into the crystal.

When the crystal begins to glow with a grey mist, take it in your hands; imagine its power being drawn into your body.

Close your eyes, repeating your wish as you turn the crystal in your hands. Shape your wish into the crystal until you feel it glow with warmth.

Replace the crystal on the velvet. Cover it with rose petals. Leave it for three days and three nights.

To attract wealth

This spell should be worked seven hours after a New Moon.

you will require
* two turquoise-coloured candles
* a small dish or incense burner
* a charcoal block
* some sweet-smelling incense
* a small turquoise stone
* seven silver coins
* a sheet of silver paper
* a photograph of yourself
* a few drops of musk oil

Light the charcoal block in the dish and blow it into an ember.

Kneel before the altar and, before lighting the candles, anoint them slowly and quite methodically with the musk oil, saying as

you do so: 'Gods of abundance and prosperity, I ask for these to come to me.'

Light the candles, and on the smouldering charcoal block, add a little sweet incense and a few drops of musk oil. In the centre of the silver paper place your photograph. On top of it, put the turquoise stone and around it the seven silver coins.

Hold your hands over the articles and repeat the above spell seven times. Fold up the silver paper and make a small parcel. Pass the parcel through each candle seven times quickly, then lay it on the altar and repeat the spell once more.

Leave the parcel on the altar undisturbed for seven days and seven nights. After this time, place it in a drawer which is seldom opened.

TO ENCOURAGE GENEROSITY
IN SOMEONE

This spell should be carried out seven nights after a New Moon.

you will require
* two red candles
* a small dish or incense burner
* a charcoal block
* some sweet-smelling incense
* a red rose
* some cinnamon powder
* a red pen
* a piece of parchment paper
* seven silver coins
* if possible, a photograph of the person to be influenced

Light the charcoal block in the dish and blow it into an ember. Placed a candle on each side of the mirror.

On the smouldering charcoal block, sprinkle some sweet incense and half a teaspoonful of cinnamon.

Prop the photograph of the person against the mirror and write his or her name on the parchment paper. Place on top of it the silver coins and the red rose, hold the palms of your hands over the parchment paper, and say: 'With these coins, the spirit I invoke: to give and receive as the words that are spoke.'

Leave the articles on the altar undisturbed for seven days and seven nights.

VI

spells for
health & well-being

THE WITCH BOTTLE

If you are depressed and in low spirits and can discover no reason for this state of mind, it may be that negative influences are being directed against you as a result of jealousy, etc. A way to protect yourself against these is to utilize this ancient witch remedy.

This spell can be worked at any phase of the Moon.

you will require
  ∗ a screwtop jar half-filled with vinegar
  ∗ a lock of your hair
  ∗ a few nail parings
  ∗ a scattering of rosemary needles

Sprinkle on the vinegar the hair, nail parings and rosemary needles.

Seal the jar. Tie a red ribbon around it with a bow on top and place it under your bed.

To have questions
answered in a dream

This spell can be worked at any phase of the Moon.

Using two squares of purple velvet, fashion a small pillow. Stuff it with equal amounts of mugwort (a herb used to heighten awareness and produce visions) and lavender.

Before sleeping, clearly voice aloud three times your question and place the pillow so that you inhale the perfume. A dream will answer your query.

TO SEEK SPIRITUAL GROWTH AND CREATIVITY

This spell should be carried out on the night of a New Moon.

you will require
- ∗ two purple candles
- ∗ a small dish or incense burner
- ∗ a charcoal block
- ∗ some sweet-smelling incense
- ∗ three pine cones
- ∗ a bowl of rainwater
- ∗ a few red rose petals

Light the charcoal block and blow it into an ember. Once it smoulders, add some sweet incense.

Light the candles, kneel before the altar, close your eyes and meditate silently on what you wish to achieve. Do this for about ten minutes.

Gaze into the bowl containing the water and allow your gaze to drift until you see patterns forming in the water.

Place the pine cones in the water and scatter the rose petals around them, saying as you do so: 'Unfold my path towards the light. Unfold my gifts to deepen sight.'

Leave the altar undisturbed for three days and three nights.

TO INCREASE DIVINATION AND SECOND SIGHT

This ritual should be worked on the night before a Full Moon.

you will require
* two purple candles
* a small dish or incense burner
* a charcoal block, lit and blown into an ember
* some sweet-smelling incense
* some mugwort
* flowers of the hawthorn bush
* powdered nutmeg
* rose essence

The ritual should be performed at a time when you are in a mood of serenity and feel able to be totally relaxed in your mind without intrusive peripheral worries.

In this mood, kneel before the altar, scatter sweet incense on the smouldering charcoal block, add three pinches of mugwort and three of powdered nutmeg.

Hold the incense close to your face and inhale the smoke deeply three times.

Anoint the candles with the rose essence from base to top carefully and imagine the area in the centre of your forehead (which is where the psychic third eye is said to be located) slowly opening.

Light the candles and place them on each side of the mirror. Gaze into the mirror, holding in your hands the hawthorn flowers and steadily inhaling their perfume.

Mentally ask a question concerning a person or situation. Concentrate on this for about five minutes, holding it in your mind, and then say aloud: 'Lady of the Moon, illumine my vision. Beyond time and space, show me the world.'

A vision will arise in the area of the third eye. To strengthen this, repeat the invocation twice more while continuing to look into the mirror, allowing your gaze to drift as a mist forms. When you eyes become heavy, let them close; the vision will become clearer.

To continue the development of this ability, repeat the ritual at the same time and on the night before the Full Moon each month. When hawthorn flowers are no longer available, marigold or powdered mace and essence of lemon grass can be substituted.

To become invisible

Because we sense and are sensed by other people, the secret of invisibility lies in suspending mental activity. This ritual gives the ability to move around unnoticed. It should be carried out three nights before a Full Moon.

you will require
* one white candle, placed before the mirror on the altar
* Mystic Veil oil

Anoint the candle before lighting it with Mystic Veil oil. Kneel before the altar, gaze into the mirror and imagine your reflection fading. Concentrate on suspension of thought by thinking of black velvet. As the candle burns, anoint yourself with the Mystic Veil oil on your forehead, your palms, your chest and your feet. Then, still concentrating, go to where you do not wish to be seen.

To remove malignant influences

If you believe someone is directing jealous or evil thoughts towards you, this spell will counteract the evil and protect you. It should be carried out on the night of a New Moon.

you will require
* two white candles
* a small dish or incense burner
* a charcoal block
* some sweet-smelling incense
* a sharp knife
* half a cup of rainwater
* a teaspoonful of olive oil
* seven whole cloves
* the petals of two white roses
* a small bowl

First, light the charcoal block. When it is smouldering, add to it some sweet incense.

With the tip of the sharp knife, scratch into each candle your full name, place one on either side of the mirror, then light them.

Mix the water and olive oil together in the bowl, dip your fingers into the oil and water and anoint the candles, first the left, then the right, saying as you do: 'May the purity of this white light protect me from evil.'

Pick up the cloves, one at a time by the stem end, hold briefly in the candle flame and immediately drop them in the water and oil.

At midnight, pour the oil and clove mixture into the earth.

Scatter the rose petals on the earth and leave without looking back.

To remove misfortune

Inevitably on life's path, we all experience a bad run of luck or misfortune. To bring it to an end, this spell should be performed three days after a Full Moon.

you will require
- two black candles, one placed each side of the mirror
- three small jars, with lids
- nine garlic cloves
- vinegar
- a few white rose petals
- nine new, unused pins

Kneel before the altar, hold the garlic cloves in the palms of your hand and meditate on the misfortunes either in your own life or that of the friend or loved one on whose behalf you are working the spell. Then say aloud: 'May misfortune retreat, and good luck repeat. Into this garlic be evil devoured, by the strength of light be empowered.'

Stick a pin in each of the garlic cloves and place three in each jar. Cover them with the vinegar and add two white rose petals to each jar.

Firmly close the lids, and on the same night as working the spell, throw the jars into a fast-flowing river.

A SPELL TO ALLEVIATE A TEMPORARY DEPRESSION

This spell should be carried out on the first night after a New Moon.

you will require

* one yellow and one green candle, placed before the mirror so that their light is reflected
* a small dish or incense burner
* a charcoal block
* myrrh incense
* vanilla essence

Light the charcoal block and blow it into an ember. When it smoulders, sprinkle on some myrrh incense and a few drops of vanilla essence.

Kneel at the altar, gaze into the mirror and meditate on your low spirits for about five minutes.

Place your right hand around the yellow candle and say: 'Spirits of Sun and Light, embrace my heart and make it bright.'

Imagine the warmth of sunlight around you, lifting your mood. Place your left hand around the green candle and say: 'Spirits of Nature and Growth, renew my energy and help me to rise and flow with life.'

Feel the healing energies of Nature around you and give thanks for their bounties.

A CHARM TO GIVE A FRIEND
TO PROMOTE HEALING

The charm should be prepared on your altar
on the night of a New Moon.

you will require
* two blue candles
* a small dish or incense burner
* a charcoal block
* sweet-smelling incense
* a photograph of your friend
* a small carnelian stone,
  to promote health
* a few oak leaves, for strength
* some lavender, for tranquillity
* a whole marigold flower, to represent
  the life-giving properties of the Sun
* a small blue drawstring bag to hold the
  charm (made by hand or machine or
  purchased from a supplier)

Light the charcoal block and blow it into an ember. Light the candles. Scatter sweet incense on the smouldering charcoal block. Place the photograph before the mirror.

The charm contents should he carefully placed on the photograph and left with the burning candles for one hour. At the end of this time, kneel before the altar, place your hands over the photograph and say: 'Health of the soul, health of the body, refresh my friend (Name) and restore him/her to perfect wholeness.'

Place the charm contents carefully in the bag and close the drawstring. Pass the bag briefly through the candle on the left, then the right, and finally through the smoke of the incense. Give the bag to your friend with instructions to keep it with him/her at all times.

A HEALING SPELL

This spell should be carried out three nights before a Full Moon. You should have on your altar a clean white cloth and fresh flowers in a vase of water; flowers represent the gift of life.

you will require
- ✳ two blue candles, one placed on each side of the mirror
- ✳ a small dish or incense burner
- ✳ a charcoal block
- ✳ sweet-smelling incense
- ✳ a few yew needles
- ✳ a blue pen (blue is the colour of healing)
- ✳ a photograph of the person to be healed
- ✳ a freshly laid egg

Light the charcoal block and blow it into an ember. Place the photograph in the middle of the altar. Sprinkle some incense on the smouldering charcoal block, then add a few yew needles. Yew trees live to a great age and reflect longevity.

Kneel before the altar, gaze into the mirror and mentally build an image of the sick person as strong, healthy and full of vigour. Hold this picture in your mind as you take the egg into your hands and carefully write the full name of the person to be healed on the surface of the egg. Repeat until the complete surface of the egg is covered.

Lay the egg carefully on the photograph and leave it there until the night of the Full Moon. At that time, place the egg in a paper bag and take it to a swiftly flowing river. Hold the bag between your hands, crush the egg and throw the bag into the river and leave without turning back.

TO STOP THE SPREAD OF MALICIOUS GOSSIP

This spell should be carried out on the night of a Waning Moon.

you will require
- one black candle, placed before the mirror on your altar so that its light is reflected
- a small dish or incense burner
- a charcoal block
- a piece of plain white paper
- a black pen
- a supply of the herb wormwood

Kneel before the altar and write on the paper the names of the people, if known, who are spreading the gossip. If unknown, simply write a question mark.

Sprinkle some of the wormwood on the smouldering charcoal block. Hold your hands above the names and repeat nine times: 'Evil tongues, vicious and free, be bound and silenced by three times three.'

Sprinkle wormwood in a circle around the names and leave on the altar for nine days and nine nights. At the end of that time, destroy the paper by burning and allow the ashes to be carried away by the four winds.

House-moving spell

Before moving from your house to a new home, use this spell to spiritually cleanse your old and new homes.

you will require
* a branch cut from a willow tree to make a small wand
* two yellow candles
* a small dish containing water from a spring
* a little salt

Place the salt and the dish containing the water on the altar. Light the candles and place them on each side of the mirror. Meditate, gazing into the mirror, on the positive energies and memories of your home.

Sprinkle some salt into the water, saying: 'I endow this water with purity and peace. May peace and happiness prevail in this home.' Then, carrying the wand and the dish with the water, dip the wand into the water periodically and sprinkle it around doors, windows and walls as you move through each room in a clockwise direction.

When you reach your new home, carry out this spell there as you visualize the happiness you anticipate there.

A ritual of thanksgiving

As the gods grant our wishes and desire that we should be happy, we should remember to give them thanks for the blessings of our lives, for life itself, health, love, family, and friends, and for the beautiful world that we inhabit with its myriad wonders. Remembering that what we project into the world is reflected towards us, the gods will look favourably on those who are grateful for their gifts.

This ritual can be performed on any night from a New Moon to a Full Moon. A vase of white flowers should be on the altar placed in front of the mirror, and petals of flowers scattered on the altar and on the floor around the altar.

you will require
* two white candles, for the altar
* four white candles (or small night lights) to be placed in the east, south, west and north on the floor around the altar
* a small dish or incense burner
* a charcoal block
* sweet-smelling incense

for the casting

Light the charcoal block and blow it into an ember. Light the altar candles and place them on each side of the mirror.

Scatter sweet incense on the smouldering charcoal block, and then light the quarter candles on the floor.

Kneel before the altar and gaze into the mirror, close your eyes and for a few minutes, contemplate the blessings of your life, remembering blessings not often considered: the ability to see, hear, to speak and to walk.

Take up the incense burner and, starting in the east, hold it up to the gods and say aloud: 'Great Mother of the Gods, Lady of the Moon, Giver of Life and Love, I tender thanks to you for the blessings of my life so freely bestowed. May the souls of all beings be enfolded in peace, harmony, health and love, and may your glorious light shine always, enriching Holy Earth with your presence.'

Repeat the invocation with the incense at the three other quarters. Return the incense to the altar. Allow the candles to burn for one hour.

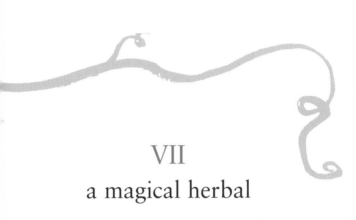

VII
a magical herbal

Asafoetida
A purifying herb. Disposes of evil and disappointments.

Basil
Promotes calmness, healing and protection from illness.

Bay leaf
Used to invoke visions and wishes.

Bitter aloes
Used to negate love.

Cedar oil
Used in conjunction with garlic. Protects and preserves.

Cinnamon
Promotes passion and generosity.

Cloves
Disposes of hostile, negative forces.

Dragon's blood
Gives energy to spells. Also used for
general protection.

Garlic
An antidote to evil in thought and action.

Geranium
Promotes protection, healing and reconciliation.

Eucalyptus
Used for the holding of positive attitudes
and intentions.

Hawthorn
With the element of fire, represents endings.

Honey
Induces sweetness to relationships and wishes.

Horse chestnut
Attracts and assists in the exchange of business matters.

Ivy
With its clinging properties, ivy promotes faithfulness.

Lavender
Used for healing, calmness, relaxation and peace.

Leaves of the ash tree
Used to remove obstacles.

Leaves of the oak tree
Represents strength and renewal.

Marjoram
Calms and cleanses.

Musk
Promotes fundamentals, abundance, health
and happiness.

Nutmeg
Used to cement love, friendship and understanding;
also aids clairvoyance.

Olive oil
Cleanses and purifies.

Patchouli oil
Represents the sweetness of love.

Pine cones
Represent fertility of mind and body.

Rose
Protects and strengthens love.

Rosemary
A vitalizing herb. Aids mental powers, promotes
self-assurance, stimulates memory.

Rue
Protects against egotism, envy, aids the healing of
these and counteracts inertia.

Sage
Promotes relaxation and healing.

Thyme
Used for renewal and encouragement.

Vanilla
Promotes love and passion.

Walnuts
Encourage prosperity.

Wormwood
A herb of protection.

Index

160 *spells to change your life*